Oregon

By Susan Labella

Subject Consultant
George H. Taylor
State Climatologist for Oregon
Oregon State University
Corvallis, Oregon

Reading Consultant
Cecilia Minden-Cupp, PhD
Former Director of the Language and Literacy Program
Harvard Graduate School of Education
Cambridge, Massachusetts

Children's Press®
A Division of Scholastic Inc.
New York   Toronto   London   Auckland   Sydney
Mexico City   New Delhi   Hong Kong
Danbury, Connecticut

Designer: Herman Adler Design
Photo Researcher: Caroline Anderson
The photo on the cover shows a bridge in downtown Portland, Oregon.

Library of Congress Cataloging-in-Publication Data

Labella, Susan, 1948–
  Oregon / by Susan Labella.
    p. cm. — (Rookie read-about geography)
  Includes index.
  ISBN-10: 0-516-25386-7 (lib. bdg.)   0-531-16785-2 (pbk.)
  ISBN-13: 978-0-516-25386-2 (lib. bdg.)   978-0-531-16785-4 (pbk.)
  1. Oregon—Juvenile literature. 2. Oregon—Geography—Juvenile literature.
I. Title. II. Series.
  F876.3.L33 2006
  979.5—dc22   2005024567

CHILDREN'S PRESS, and ROOKIE READ-ABOUT®,
and associated logos are trademarks and/or registered trademarks
of Scholastic Library Publishing. SCHOLASTIC and associated logos
are trademarks and/or registered trademarks of Scholastic Inc.
1 2 3 4 5 6 7 8 9 10 R 16 15 14 13 12 11 10 09 08 07

Do you know why Oregon
is called the Beaver State?

A beaver swims past its dam.

Many beavers live in the rivers in Oregon.

Beavers build dams from tree branches and mud. The dams hold back water and protect the beavers from other animals.

Oregon is in the
northwestern part of
the United States.

Can you find Oregon on
this map?

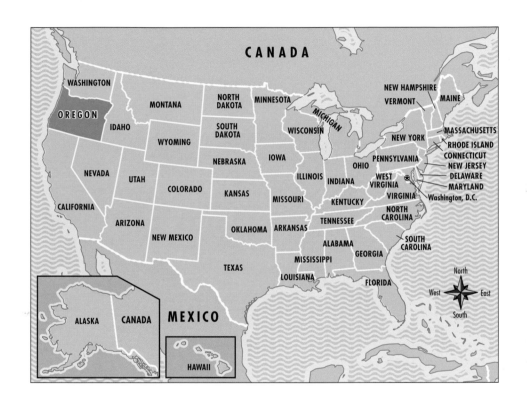

CANADA

WASHINGTON
OREGON
IDAHO
MONTANA
NORTH DAKOTA
MINNESOTA
SOUTH DAKOTA
WYOMING
NEBRASKA
IOWA
WISCONSIN
MICHIGAN
NEVADA
UTAH
COLORADO
KANSAS
CALIFORNIA
ARIZONA
NEW MEXICO
OKLAHOMA
ARKANSAS
MISSOURI
ILLINOIS
INDIANA
OHIO
KENTUCKY
TENNESSEE
WEST VIRGINIA
PENNSYLVANIA
NEW YORK
VERMONT
NEW HAMPSHIRE
MAINE
MASSACHUSETTS
RHODE ISLAND
CONNECTICUT
NEW JERSEY
DELAWARE
MARYLAND
VIRGINIA
Washington, D.C.
NORTH CAROLINA
SOUTH CAROLINA
GEORGIA
ALABAMA
MISSISSIPPI
LOUISIANA
TEXAS
FLORIDA

ALASKA CANADA

MEXICO

HAWAII

North
West East
South

7

People enjoy fly-fishing in Oregon's rivers.

Oregon has many outdoor activities. Its rivers are great for white-water rafting and fly-fishing.

Crater Lake is in southwest Oregon. It is the deepest lake in the United States.

People who visit the lake can fish or scuba dive in its clear, blue water.

The Cascade Mountains run through western Oregon. These mountains are perfect for skiing and snowboarding.

Mount Hood rises more than 11,000 feet (3,000 meters) in the Cascade Mountains. It is the highest point in Oregon.

A Douglas fir grows on an Oregon mountainside.

Forests cover much of Oregon. The state tree is the Douglas fir.

Tall cedar, spruce, and hemlock trees grow near the coast.

Oregon has miles of beach
and sand dunes along the
Pacific Ocean.

Sea lions live along the rocky coast.

The Oregon grape is Oregon's state flower.

Colorful flowers grow
on Oregon's coast.
The state flower is the
Oregon grape.

Farmers in Oregon grow many kinds of fruits and vegetables. Eastern Oregon is good for growing wheat and potatoes.

An Oregon wheat field

Some Oregon farmers grow pears.

Farmers in western Oregon
grow pears, cherries,
peaches, and beans.

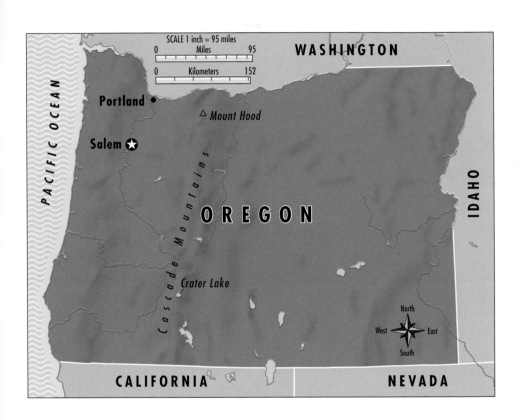

Salem is the capital
of Oregon. The Oregon
State Fair takes place in
Salem every year. Visitors
enjoy contests, music,
and many different kinds
of food.

Portland is the largest city in Oregon. It is famous for its many rose gardens. Some people even call Portland the Rose City.

The Portland Rose Festival is held there every year. This festival includes parades, fireworks, and beautiful flowers.

The Portland Rose Festival features parades with colorful floats.

Young visitors sail a kite along Oregon's rocky coast.

Oregon is an exciting place to visit!

What will you do first when you visit?

Words You Know

beaver

Cascade Mountains

Crater Lake

Douglas fir

Mount Hood

Oregon grape flowers

Pacific Ocean

sea lions

Index

About the Author

Susan Labella is a former teacher and editor. She is currently a freelance writer and has written other books in the Rookie Read-About® Geography series.

Photo Credits

Photographs © 2007: Alamy Images/Chuck Pefley: 23; Corbis Images: cover (Richard Cummins), 16, 30 bottom right (Paul A. Souders); Danita Delimont Stock Photography/Janis Miglavs: 8, 28; David R. Frazier: 18; Dembinsky Photo Assoc.: 3, 30 top left (Dominique Braud), 15, 31 top left (David J. Littell); Nature Picture Library Ltd./Jeff Foott: 4; Photo Researchers, NY: 20, 31 top right (Dennis Flaherty), 19, 31 bottom right (Tom & Pat Leeson), 11, 30 bottom left (George Ranalli); Portland Rose Festival Association/Dick Powers: 27, 31 bottom left; Ric Ergenbright: 12, 22, 30 top right.

Maps by Bob Italiano